Dancing with Butterflies
Discovering Mindfulness Through Breathing

Library of Congress Control Number: 2020910473

ISBN: (paperback): 9798655229174
ISBN: (hardback): 978-1-952733-05-5
ISBN: (eBook): 978-1-952733-07-9

To my little dancer, Leah.

You are my greatest gift. I am so grateful that I
was chosen to nurture you through life's journey.
I admire the strength that you have within you and
your artistic nature. I love you at every stage of life,
and I am excited to see the woman you'll become.
I will forever be proud to be your mom.

To those who are dealing with their butterflies:

Let's face it, whether you're a kid or a grown-up,
some feelings can be confusing and scary,
causing those butterflies to swirl in your belly.
They seem to appear out of nowhere and can be hard
to navigate, but it is possible. Taking a moment
to still your body and mind can help you think
clearly about the things you are worried about.
Doing the breathing exercises Leah and her mom did for a
longer time is called meditation. It is an amazing way to
start your day and it doesn't have to take long.
Spending 5 to 10 minutes in the morning or evening is
something you can do with your family. You can find a nice,
quiet place and play some soothing music, or go online
and find a short-guided meditation. Go forward and
conquer butterflies and drums every day, together.

Send me pictures of you and your little one
breathing to my social media
@Author Adrienne Barr on Facebook.
I would love to see them!

All Leah wants to do is dance.

She had found her passion, that one thing she could do all day, every day.

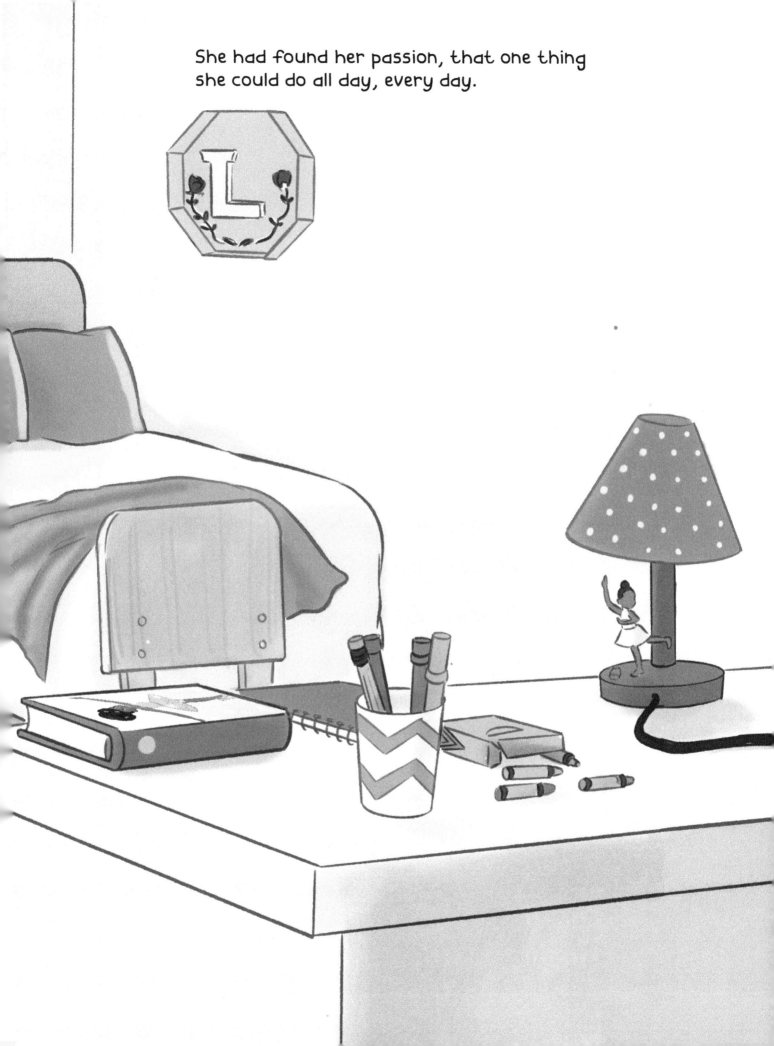

Leah loved bending, stretching, twirling, jumping, and gracefully moving to music.

Leah's dance teacher, Ms. Dora, would help her learn new moves two days a week.

At home, Leah's mom would play music so Leah could dance around and practice her moves.

Leah loved to dance in front of the long mirror in the hallway. She felt so free.

Leah would close her eyes and imagine she was dancing on stage with big, bright lights shining on her and the audience cheering.

But this time, when Leah opened her eyes and thought about all those people watching her, she began to feel something. It felt like a vacuum came and stole her air, and a drum was playing in her chest.

Leah wasn't sure if this was something she should tell her mom. She didn't want to worry her, and she thought the feeling would stop and never come back, so she kept it to herself.

The next week at practice, Ms. Dora told the class that they are having a dance recital in three weeks.

Cookie asked, "What's a recital?" Ms. Dora replied,
"A recital is when you perform in front of a crowd,
showing them what you've learned."

Leah quickly felt that funny feeling again.
It felt like something was fluttering in her tummy.
After practice was over, Leah's mom picked her up.

As they were heading home, Leah's mom asked, "So, ladybug, Ms. Dora tells me you all are going to have a recital. How are you feeling about it?"

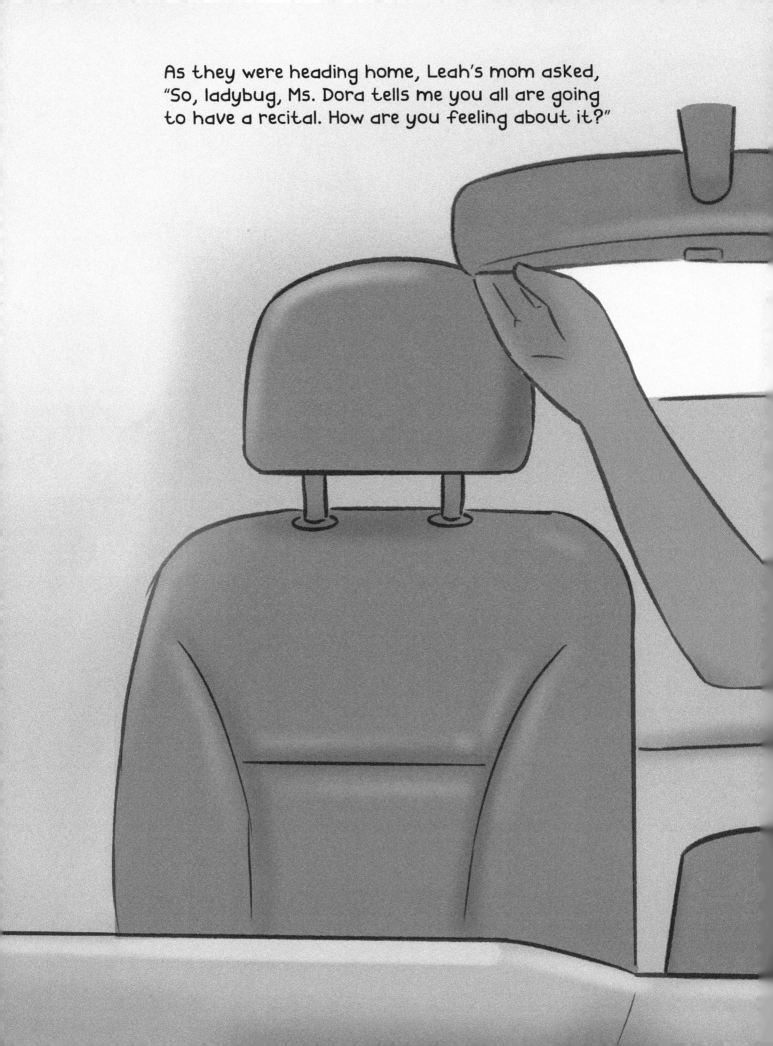

Leah had that strange feeling again, so she stayed quiet.
"What's wrong, baby?" Asked Mom.

Leah said, "Every time I think about being in front of all those people, my stomach starts to feel funny."

"Oh, honey, it sounds like you have the butterflies,"
Mom said. Leah exclaimed, "Butterflies?!
How do butterflies get in your stomach?"

Mom explained, "The butterflies are just a feeling. Those butterflies are your body's reaction to being nervous about something. It can feel like a twister of butterflies blowing around in there."

"But did you know you can calm those butterflies?"
Leah replied curiously, "How, Mommy? I have to know!
I don't like this feeling."

"If you take a deep breath and let it out slowly, the butterflies will calm down. It's like you are controlling the wind to stop the butterflies. Once they calm down, you can focus on doing whatever you have to do," Mom said.

"I want to try it!" Leah exclaimed. "Okay, honey, give it a try. I'll do it with you," Mom said. "We'll start by taking a good, deep breath, holding it in and counting to four, then slowly letting out the air and counting to four. Imagine you're blowing a dandelion. We'll do this four times. One, two, three, four."

"You can even close your eyes if you like," Mom said.
They took in another deep breath. This time,
Leah closed her eyes. Then, they let it out.
One, two, three, four.

"How do you feel, honey?" Mom asked. Leah noticed
the butterflies within her had settled.
"I feel better, Mommy! It worked!"

Later that night, after Mom had tucked her into bed and gave her goodnight kisses, Leah began to practice the breathing again. She liked the way taking those deep breaths and releasing them made her feel. Every time she inhaled, she was inhaling calm. Every time she exhaled, she was releasing anything that bothered her.

She felt like she was the princess of air, controlling each moment by just breathing. It felt so magical to her.

The day of the recital had finally come. Leah and her classmates were dressed in beautiful, long, flowing dresses and were waiting on the sides of the stage.

Leah peeked out to see if she could find where her mom was sitting, but all she saw was a sea of people. Instantly, the butterflies in her stomach began to put on their own show.

"Oh no!" Leah thought. "There's so many people, and the butterflies are back!"

Just then, Ms. Dora announced it was time to go on stage. "Go do your best. All of you will do great!" She said.

Leah felt like the butterflies were walking her on stage instead of her feet. Her hands got sweaty, and the drums began playing in her chest again. Her legs began wobbling with the drums.

"There is so much going on! What do I do about these butterflies and drums?" Leah thought. Just as Leah walked to her spot, she saw her mom in the front row. Mom smiles and motions for her to breathe.

"Oh, that's right!" Leah thought. "I can calm them down!"
Leah took a deep breath and let it out slowly.

She could still feel those butterflies. Leah closed her eyes and took another deep breath, then let the air out slowly. One, two, three, four. She did this another two times, imagining herself gently blowing a dandelion. She felt calm and at home in her body, confident that she could dance carefree. It worked!

The music and lights come on and Leah and her classmates begin to dance. Leah dances with grace, not missing a beat. Her arms stretched toward the ceiling, and her legs and feet kept perfect time with the routine and music.

Leah realized that breathing helped her clear her mind so she could perform and have fun in the moment. Once the dance was over, the crowd stood up and cheered. Leah looked at her mom, and they smiled at each other. Mom blew her kisses and continued cheering.

Leah was so proud of herself. She calmed those fluttery butterflies, stopped the beating drums, and danced beautifully on stage.
She felt like she could do anything!

Adrienne Barr, a proud single mother,
earned a Bachelor of Arts in Communications
with a minor in Telecommunications at
Johnson C. Smith University. Adrienne often jokes
that her daughter earned the degree with her,
as she had her daughter a few months before
she graduated. She enjoys doing community
service, spending time with family and friends,
and various other activities in the
Triad area of North Carolina.

CPSIA information can be obtained
at www.ICGtesting.com
Printed in the USA
LVHW070829100920
665516LV00030B/485